"50" WAYS
TO USE FEMININE
HYGIENE PRODUCTS
IN A MANLY MANNER
(FOR THE SELF-ASSURED MALE)

BY: B. KOZ

Copyright © 2008 by B. Koz

ISBN 0-7414-4889-0

Published by:

PUBLISHING.COM

1094 New DeHaven Street, Suite 100
West Conshohocken, PA 19428-2713
Info@buybooksontheweb.com
www.buybooksontheweb.com
Toll-free (877) BUY BOOK
Local Phone (610) 941-9999
Fax (610) 941-9959

Printed in the United States of America

Printed on Recycled Paper

Published March 2010

FOREWORD

Before you read any further, please ask yourself if you are a very self-assured manly male. If the answer is no, put the book down and back away.

The applications for these products as they apply to the uses other than their known purposes, will be very embarrassing to a non-self-assured male. Take all applicable uses described in this book (manual) with a grain of salt.

Men, we all know we never know when Mr. P, formally known as "my period", will come into our lives. It is, however, usually at the most inconvenient times right?! How many times in our lives are we going to hear those dreaded words, "Honey, not now, I'm on my period". Well guys, at these times of the month, you have a little extra time on your hands, right? Use this time wisely to get your "manly" stuff in order and have some laughs. We all know when Mr. P's in town, laughs are hard to come by.

Enjoy the read and keep it handy as a reference manual next to your toolbox.

Have you heard the one, "How many tampons does it take to clean three bowling balls?" The answer (also included later in the book) is "one". One tampon can clean nine finger holes, except if your balls are extremely dirty.

The application of feminine products described in this manual have been tested and used by me many times prior to the thought of writing a book. Some I have used for more than thirty years.

Know one thing: the cheaper the pads, the less they stick. Buy the top of the line. Nothing could be more embarrassing then using an inferior pad while attempting to be that manly male.

Did you know that they can produce a mini/maxi pad in 40 seconds? That is from start to finish, wrapped in plastic and boxed.

The layout of this manual is based on the order of manly applications starting with hunting and ending with how to treat a woman, not that this isn't manly.

Now let's get to the manly meat of this book and learn a couple of tricks you can use in the real world as a self-assured male.

TABLE OF CONTENTS

I.

Sports/

Hunting/

Guns

GUN CLEANING – #1

Gun Cleaning: Tampons
(The size depends on the gauge of your shot gun).

Try different sizes and find the ones that are the snuggest in the barrel and buy a box. Yes men, we CAN buy tampons if we're self-assured males. Keep a couple with your guns just in case, as I did, you forget your gun cleaning kit on a weekend getaway.

We shot skeet all day and that night I wanted to clean my gun…no kit. The only thing in the cabin long enough to go the length of the barrel were my arrows. Now I needed a cleaning pad. I looked through some drawers and found some tampons. I slid the tampon out about 1 inch and applied some solvent. These things really expand quickly and that is why you should only expose about an inch. Now insert it into the barrel holding onto the applicator and push the string side with the arrow. Don't push it all the way through because you won't get it back in. Work it back and forth a few times then push string side out, grab the string and discard. Your hands shouldn't even get solvent on them.

For semi-automatics, same applies but you need to extend the string in order to pull it out the end of the barrel. I use large, heavy days on my 12 gauge Weatherby over/under.

GUN STOCK PROTECTION/
2 CASE GUNS – #2

Gun Stock Protection: Self-Adhesive Mini Pads.

If you have ever used a case that holds 2 guns, you probably experienced this. You get to the location to shoot and when you open the case, to your horror, the 2 guns have been rubbing against each other the whole trip. The nicest one, your favorite gun, is usually the one with the damage – a scratched stock.

Before the trip home, peel and stick a mini pad on one or both contact areas. This will keep them looking good and prevent them from looking old before their time.

Note: Keep your guns guys! They don't cost you any money unless you shoot them and they don't yell at you. Let them sit in their case in the closet and they do what you want them to do when the time comes for them to perform. What more could you ask for on this planet?

GUN CLEANING – #3

Cleaning Outside the Barrel – Light Day Panty Shields.

When your friends handle your gun like they handle themselves, tell them to keep their hands and finger prints off the barrel of your gun. This will cause acid imprints on the barrel if you don't clean it until the next time out shooting.

Do not take just any rag that is lying around to wipe the barrel clean. Instead grab one of your wife's or girlfriend's Light Day Panty Shields and use that to clean the outside of the barrel. Stick one on your hand, because you're a manly man, and spray some solvent onto it and go about cleaning your gun or guns that your friends have felt up during the day or weekend.

Guys, when a rag gets WD-40 or whatever you put on it, you must throw it away, correct? A mini pad is much easier to discard than a shop towel. It will light up like you put it in gas. That solvent or WD-40 is very flammable. Caution…don't light the woods on fire. Be very aware of what you are doing, ok?

GUN BUTT PADDING - #4

**Skeet Shooting – Self-Adhesive Maxi Pads (Thick),
or Multi-layers of Mini Pads.**

Have you ever been skeet or target shooting with a female that will not participate in the fun because she's afraid that the butt of the gun will hurt or bruise her shoulder and you don't have a rubber slide on pad handy? Keep some pads in your ammo case. Lay the pad on a flat surface, adhesive side up, then place the butt of the gun on it and trace it. Trim excess material off to prevent snagging. Peel and stick and let her burn some lead too. She'll be impressed that you wanted her to have fun too. The same applies to mini pads, but you will have to layer them to the thickness she prefers.

CHEEK PROTECTION #5

Cheek Protection for Females – Self-Adhesive Mini Pad.

If you're like me, I want to burn a lot of lead in an afternoon like maybe 400 rounds of skeet loads at one time. Unfortunately, this will cause some irritation to your face and even more so if you're shooting with a female. Where your cheeks, no not those cheeks, come into contact with the stock, place a self-adhesive mini pad on the stock. This will keep your female partner from looking like you beat her before dinner. Believe me; a female's face does bruise much easier than us males. Also, this will keep their makeup off the stock of your prized possession. You may go through women, but not too many guns. If you're like me, I've been through 4 women, but I still have my Ithica and Weatherby. They are a foundation us men must carry with us until we die.

INSIDE HEEL OF
HUNTING BOOTS – #6

Heel Felt of Hunting Boots – Self-Adhesive Pads.

The size of pad you use depends on the area to be covered. This one I used on a hunting trip miles from the nearest store. The felts in my boots, right behind the heel, wore out and my heel was rubbing against rubber causing blisters. When I got back to the cabin, I looked through the drawers and found that my wife had a supply of pads. I thought that if I peeled one and stuck the adhesive part on the rubber it would give me enough padding to go out for the evening hunt. I did not end up buying new felts until I got home.

BOOT CUSHION – #7

Side of Boot Cushion – Self-Adhesive Pad.

To shield the area of the shoe or boot that is causing your discomfort, this extra cushion is a life saver if you are miles from a store. You can go about hunting or hiking until you get the proper fix. Cut a pad in the shape of the area where the discomfort is. Be sure not to cut off the adhesive part. Adhere it to the inside of the boot and keep on hiking.

SOLE PADS – HIKING BOOTS – #8

Sole Pads – Self-Adhesive Mini Pads.

If you're going out for a day hike, pack some mini pads in your backpack. During the hike if the soles of your feet start getting sore, peel and stick the pads to the inside sole of your boots. You will not believe the difference depending on the thickness of the pads you're using. You should have a knife, or better yet, a pair of small cuticle scissors on you to trim the pad for a perfect fit.

II.

Mechanical/

Motorcycle

Prepping

MOTORCYLE PREPPING - #9

Motorcycle Axle Cleaner – Tampons.

The size of the tampon depends on the size of your bike and the axle diameter.

This is one that I discovered on my own in 1978 when I was using a screw driver and a rag to get the sand and dirt out of my rear axle hub after riding the sand dunes in northern Michigan.

What came to mind was scoring my hub with the screw driver. Another problem was the rag would not go through the hub very good.

I stopped and took a break, which means, walk away and don't get so pissed off at what you're trying to do. I went in the cabin to chill out and, since I cut my hand pulling the rear tire off, I went to look for a bandage and there I came across the tampons in the drawer along with the bandages I was originally looking for. Boom! It hit me. I could use these things in a "manly manner".

I took one to see if it would fit in my hub of my 250 and, guess what, a perfect fit. I put cleaning solvent on it and inserted it in the hub, perfect fit. I did, however, put too much solvent on it and when I pushed it all the way through, it expanded too much to insert it again. I reloaded with another one and worked it back and forth until I knew it was toast and did it again with another fresh one.

Since that day, when I prep my bike, I use this idea to clean the axle hubs. It works just like cleaning a 12 gauge shot gun bore.

You better be a self-assured male when you're riding buddies come into the garage and see a box of tampons next to your bike! You can get one up on them by stating, "Do you idiots still use a rag and screw driver to clean your hubs?" Pass this tip on to save a motorcycle from the pain.

RIM CLEANER – #10

Motorcycle Rim Cleaner – Maxi Preferred.

You manly men can polish your rims by adhering a maxi pad (mini pads will work too) to your hand. Don't tear your fingers off while your prized possession is on its stand. Fire the bitch up and let it idle in first gear. Take the maxi pad coated with your preferred cleaning polish and hold it against the rim. This is a quick and simple solution for nice looking rims, but keep your fingers out of the spokes guys. I don't want to be sued over this one. Make it look good for that fox that's waiting for you in the pits. Even if you come in tenth place, you can still hit a home run back at your "Tampon Bouquet Palace" you call home for the time being. You never know, Mr. P. might blow into town on the way back from the track, but being the manly man, you will be prepared. The glove box linings will at least get you home from that four hour trip.

SPARK PLUG CLEANER – #11

Spark Plug Orifice Cleaner – Tampon Light Days.

All men have at least one thing in their life that requires a spark plug. So the next time you remove the plug, check the spark plug head orifice for carbon build up and dirt. If it is covered in dark soot, use a tampon (light days) and push it out of the applicator 2" and cut the end of it to create a point like an arrow head. Dip or spray the tip with carb cleaner and, using the applicator so not to get solvent on your hands, twist the tampon in as though you were installing a spark plug. Work it in and out a few times. This will clean the threads and make replacing the spark plug much easier. You'll be able to screw the plug in with your fingers all the way and you'll just have to snug it up with your ratchet. This is better than having to ratchet the plug all the way in, plus you'll avoid pushing all that carbon and dirt into the cylinder. We all know that's not good for the piston and cylinder.

MOTORCYCLE CRANK CASE – #12

Motorcycle Crank Case Dirt Shield –
Self-Adhesive Maxi Pads

When pulling the (jug) cylinder assembly off, peel and stick a couple of pads. This is better than a shop towel. This application will prove how self-assured you really are. Plus, it will be superior to a rag by preventing moisture from getting into the crank case. They do absorb a lot of moisture.

SOCKET CLEANER – #13

Deep Well Socket Cleaner – Tampon (light or heavy).

We've all done wrenching on something greasy and dirty and after the job is complete, your sockets are filled with that stuff. You grab a rag and screw driver and try to get it clean. One tampon can clean a whole set of deep wells. Different size tampons can be used for the different size sockets you are cleaning. Take the tampon and push it out 1" then dip it into cleaner or gas. Do I have to explain any further? We all should know by now how to clean a socket.

When the tip is dirty, push it out another 1", cut the dirty end off and keep on going.

These are the type of tips that make this manual a reference piece that should be next to your toolbox, due to the fact that we males will never remember 50 ways to use these products off the top of our heads. Let's be real guys!

SWEAT ABSORBER – #14

Moto-Cross Sweat Absorber –
Self-Adhesive Mini/Heavy Day.

In 1976, I was 16 years old and didn't have a clue about feminine products. I was pitted next to an old guy; he must have been 30 years old, Ha! At the time, that was old to me. When we got back to the pits, I saw him peel something out of his helmet, so I inquired what that was. He looked at me as though I was an idiot. "It's a mini pad," he stated. It was like 90 degrees that day and the sweat was running down inside my goggles, burning into my eyes. He gave me one to use before the next moto.

He stated that these things absorb a lot of fluid and you'll be able to see throughout the whole moto. Needless to say, it worked, and that was the first time I ever used a female hygiene product in a manly manner.

It took me 30 years to put these tips on paper, but that's where it all started.

SHIN PADS – #15

Shin Pads Moto-Cross/Trail Riding – Maxi Pads.

If you show up at a buddy's place for the weekend and they talk you into riding a dirt bike, take my advice, you're not going to be leading the pack. You will get hit with rocks, roost, and whatever is on that trail. If you don't want to be in pain the rest of the weekend, follow these instructions. Go to your trunk where you should have maxi and mini pads stored, don't tell anyone, but adhere two maxi pads over your knee caps and shins. Use tape if you have to. When that first object hits you, it will still hurt, but it shouldn't be bleeding. You'll be glad you put the pads on your shins. Believe me, I've forgot my shin pads more than once and used four maxis to cover my knees and shins. When those rocks were coming off a CR500 and hitting me, I thanked God I thought of this protection idea before I got on that bike.

VICE PADDING PROTECTION – #16

Vice Jaws Protection Padding –
Mini or Maxi Self-Adhesive.

If you work with wood or metal in any way and you've had to clamp it down to plane it or drill through it, you know about the worry of marking it up with the vise jaws. By using a mini or maxi self-adhesive pad on the jaws of the vice you can avoid this problem. This is easier than trying to hold two pieces of wood on both sides and holding the object you're clamping by yourself. I've been there and it's frustrating so I use a mini pad for most projects like this.

If you do not have a maxi pad available, you can layer a couple of the mini pads on top of each other to get the protection you need. For any idiots out there, you stick a pad on each jaw, just peel and stick them to the inside of the vice. I shouldn't have to explain this to a manly man.

SAWZALL HANDLE PADDING - #17

Vibration Padding for Sawzall Handle –
Mini/Heavy Day/Maxi.

Whenever I use a Sawzall and know it is going to be an extended amount of time, I put a mini or maxi pad around the handle. This comes from me knowing and experiencing my father's Rheumatoid Arthritis. He has hands that need as much vibration relief as anybody I know. He is too stubborn to use this idea on his Sawzall, but I did. Boy does it help holding on to that vibration assault weapon especially when I had to use it for two hours the last time. I used a maxi pad on the handle and on top of my gloves. This will give considerable relief from the vibration these things generate while you're cutting 2 x 4's out of a house. Guys, this trick means you can use your hands on something different that night.

DRILL PRESS – #18

Drill Press Table Cushions – Mini Pads.

Manly men often play with wood working projects around the house and this idea will make it a little less stressful. If you're using a drill press to drill into a piece of finished wood, adhere two mini pads on the table of your drill press. This will prevent the metal table from scratching your finished piece of wood.

This is the safest way to accomplish the task on hand and not having to worry about something getting caught up in the drill bit. I leave mine installed until I am going to drill through metal. Then I peel and throw them away till next time, and then I'll steal two more out of the "Tampon/Pad Bouquet" in the bathroom. Your wife or girlfriend won't miss them unless they are the last two in the bouquet. If that's the case, I would say, "Back away", especially if Mr. P's in town. It's not worth it guys.

DRAIN PLUG – #19

Rear Boat Drain Plug – Tampon.

Believe me or not, I swear this happened to my friend Mike and me on a cool morning on Union Lake in Michigan.

We launched his boat for the first time that year. Everything was going as planned. When we pulled away from the dock his wife asked, "What's this threaded plug for?" This is when panic set in. Mike and I argued about which one of us was going to jump into that cold water and install the plug. I won and he jumped in. The boat was taking on water fast and on his first dive to install the plug, he dropped it in 10 feet of water. Now we really have a problem. The bilge pump was not keeping up with the influx of water.

I was looking for something to plug the hole and it came to me to ask his wife if she had any tampons on board. She did. She only had two on board so we had two shots to make this work. I jumped in the water with tampon in hand. I thought about how tampons expand when they get wet, so I kept it in the applicator until I got it into position to insert it into the hole. The first attempt was a success and it expanded to the point that the bilge pump caught up with no problem.

We headed back to the dock and walked to the hardware store and bought a new plug. It was installed and we were on our way to fishing all by 9:15 a.m. One tampon saved a whole day of fishing. This prompted me to put a box on my boat, if not for a quick boat fix, but just in case Mr. P. blows into town unexpectedly. Better to be prepared than having to cut a boating trip short to go to a store on a beautiful day.

If I stated it once, I've stated it at least five times in this book, keep a supply of tampons and mini pads handy at all times. They don't take up much trunk space either.

AIR FILTER - #20

Chainsaw/Lawn Mower Air Filter –
Maxi Pad (preferably non-adhesive).

This is only an emergency repair and is not recommended for long term use by no means!

At our property in northern Michigan we are about 10 miles from town. At least 6 times a year we mow about 3 acres of grass around the cabins. There are 2 lawnmowers up there for this purpose.

Last year the foam air filter disintegrated while I was washing it out. Not having a spare one at camp, I went into the magic drawer in my cabin and grabbed a maxi pad. A mini self-adhesive pad won't work. I cut it as close to the shape of the air box and then had to remove the adhesive side of the actual pad. The adhesive would have caused restriction of the air flow.

After separating the pad, you should test it by trying to blow and suck air through it. If it is still too restricted, peel another layer off until you can blow air through it.

This will also work for a temporary fix for a chain saw. Replace the air filter ASAP after you have a chance to get to a store.

III.

Around

the House/

Cleaning

SOCK PROTECTION # 21

Sock Protection – Mini Pads.

Guys, if you're like me, I like people to take their shoes off when they come into my home, especially, when they come over after a night at the bar. All of us self-assured males know what we step in at the urinals in the bar. You would think our aim would be better after 21 years of aiming that thing between our legs.

To prevent those urine soaked shoes from coming in contact with your carpet, have on hand a box of self-adhesive mini pads. Tell them at the door to take off their shoes and put a mini pad on the bottom of their socks. You only won't get your carpet soiled, but you'll have a good laugh seeing your buddies wearing mini pads on their feet. You can tell them that this is the closest any of them are going to get to a female that night. If it wasn't true, they wouldn't be over at your place soiling your floors! When they leave, just tell them to peel and throw away.

CLEANING FLOORS - #22

Cleaning Floors – Maxi Self-Adhesive.

For the guys who don't want to get on their hands and knees because that doesn't look manly, use this tip to clean the dust build up on your wood floors. Guys, you know how quickly dust balls form in the bedroom, especially under the side of your bed.

For a quick clean up, adhere two self-adhesive maxi pads on your feet and armed with a can of furniture polish, spray the area and use your feet to polish the floor.

When you have company over that night, you won't look like a slob and your floors will be clean.

What is nice about this tip is that you don't even have to rinse out a rag or mop, just peel off the pads and discard. Now you self-assured males are ready for company that night. Hey, on top of that, you get a leg workout to tone those calf and thigh muscles to look better for your company. Win, win situation!

KNEE PROTECTION - #23

Knee Pads – Maxi Pads.

Do you have to scrub your floors for a party that's starting in an hour and can't find your knee pads? For quick and convenient knee pads grab a couple of maxi pads. Look in the closet or bathroom then peel and stick them to your knees. Toss them out after the job is completed. For you girls out there, if you're planning on wearing a dress that exposes your knees, this will keep your knees looking good for the party.

DUSTING - #24

Furniture Dusting – Mini or Maxi Pads.

Going along with the floor cleaning, you do not want to have dusty furniture either.

These are tips for quick clean ups when your date might stop by and most of us guys don't have dust rags in our place.

Same thing, adhere the pad on your hand and start polishing your furniture. This is the quickest way to dust the flat surfaces in your manly castle. Plus, no dirty rags left under the sink. Just throw the pad out when you're done.

TOILET CLEANING - #25

Toilet Cleaning (Exterior) – Mini Pad.

We men know more of this concern than our female counterparts. It's the area between the toilet seat hinge and the porcelain base. Brushes don't get under there all the time.

When you are cleaning the toilet (if that's your job), if not, pass on this tip because we men are the only ones that lift the seat exposing this area. Women only lift the seat all the way up when cleaning or getting sick, so it doesn't really bother them on a daily basis like us.

Apply cleaner to area and slide a mini pad under the hinge and, with both hands, slide the pad back and forth. Flip the pad over to clean the hinge using a polishing motion. Guys DO NOT flush the pad. If you do, you'll be glad you cleaned under that hinge when you're tearing the toilet apart.

FURNITURE PROTECTION - #26

Felt Replacement Pads – Mini Pads/Light Days
Self-Adhesive.

On this one I have to confess, I'm an idiot! I thought of this one in a deer blind last November and put it on paper, but today is January, 2007, and while I write, I lift my marble ashtray up and set it down gently so as not to scratch my table. Then I realize that the mini pad protection I thought of last year, I have not applied for my own reward.

I've done weird things on a Friday night, but never with a mini pad. I flipped the marble ashtray over and applied four pieces of mini pad to the bottom. Now the ashtray can be slid across the table with no fear of scratches.

TRANSPORTING FURNITURE - #27

Transporting Furniture In a Vehicle/Trailer –
Mini Heavy Day or Maxi Self-Adhesive.

We've all had to move someone and, in the back of a pickup, blankets can blow out and they are a pain in the ass to secure when driving at 60 MPH. This is my cure for this stressful situation: Put the furniture in your truck or trailer. Place either a mini pad or maxi pad on the contact areas of the objects you are moving. Guys when looking in your rearview mirror stressing out if that blanket blew out, it is a relief knowing that the pads are in place and if they do blow off, they're not going to cause an accident.

HOUSEHOLD PAINTING - #28

Lettering/Sign Painting – Tampon.

Tampons can be used for painting clear, clean lines for lettering. They leave no brush marks outside the letters. Simply push the tampon out of the applicator tube about 1/2" and while holding the tube, dip into your paint. Your hands won't get paint on them and you can begin your project. When it becomes saturated with paint, throw it out and grab another. There is no clean up required like a brush. Clean up adds to the time on the job. I used this one 15 years ago.

If you have to paint a new sign for your property, you don't want to be cleaning a brush out when you can just throw the tampon in the fire pit, correct?

PIPE SOUND INSULATION - #29

Noisy Pipes – Self-Adhesive Mini Pad.

If you have a couple of noisy pipes in your home, apply a mini pad between the pipes that are making the noise. Remember to adhere the sticky side to the hot side pipe, the cold side will not work. If you want to duct tape the pad in place, go at it.

REMOTE CONTROL - #30

Remote Control Holder – 2 Mini Pads.

Today while writing this manual and watching TV, I lost my remote for the last time in this bed. Then, BAM!, it hit me.

I found the remote under the bed. I retrieved 2 self-adhesive mini pads and a stapler. I peeled off the paper strips and placed them together with both adhesive sides out. Then I stapled them together using 8 staples. I attached the pads to the headboard and just to be on the safe side, I put two staples through the top and bottom of the pad. This would ensure that I wouldn't pull it off.

The reason I used mini pads was I didn't feel like wasting an hour of my day to run to the store for Velcro. It's also an unusual conversation piece.

WEATHER STRIPPING - #31

Door Weather Strips – Mini Pads.

I hate to keep bringing up the cabin I have in northern Michigan; it's all but 12 feet by 24 feet with a loft built by an Amish man, but this is where I use most of these ideas. The closest neighbor is a mile away and you are on your own up there with no stores within 6 miles. I do what I can to have no contact with people while I'm up there trying to relax and hunt or ride.

This past deer season it was cold and windy. The door of my cabin warped during the summer but I didn't realize it until 8:00 at night on a windy night in November. I heat this place with a small propane stove and it was not getting warm in there. Then I went outside to relieve myself and noticed I could see a lot of light coming from around the door jam. I had eight days left at deer camp and didn't have any foam in my cabin. I did have, however, a whole box of self-adhesive mini pads handy, thanks to my ex-wife. I retrieved that box from the top drawer which has helped me through the last couple of years. I used these pads to seal the door adhering them to the floor and door jam. I kept going outside and looking in until I couldn't see any light through the door. It took eight mini pads to stop the breeze from coming through, but boy did that help heating the place up. I do not recommend this as a permanent fix. I used them to stay warm for that night. I did go into town the next day and buy foam.

I guess I'm going to be a self-assured male and go into town and buy a box of tampons and a box of self-adhesive mini pads this coming spring. It's called restocking what you use. I'll get this out of the way before my race buddies come up in the summer.

WINDOW CONDENSATION - #32

Cabin Window Condensation – Mini Pads.

When I go up to northern Michigan to my cabin, it is heated totally off propane gas. In the winter this causes a lot of condensation to form on the windows which drips onto the sills and forms ice. I know, you are wondering how cold I keep my cabin. Well even at 70 degrees the sills are still cold enough to freeze the water especially in the window tracks. At times I have found that I needed some fresh air in the cabin and I have had to take a screw driver to chisel the ice out of the tracks. That is a pain in the ass! So now I place mini pads in the tracks so that when the moisture runs down the windows it is absorbed by the pad. Once a day when I get back from the hunt, I change them out for the next day.

If you want to use a towel or rag go at it, but mini pads burn better in a fire pit than a wet towel. Plus, it is probably a towel you want to use during your trip.

TIKI TORCH - #33

Tiki Torch Wick Replacement – Tampon Light Days.

If you ever had Tiki Torches at your cabin or house, you have experienced a lost or burnt out wick at the worst time. If you're having a party and you need all the torches lit to make the place look quaint and you are in desperate need for a replacement wick, I guarantee that if females are invited, you'll get your wick to complete the atmosphere.

If you don't have tampons in the house or cabin, shame on you! Now you have to politely ask the female guests, this is when your self-assured male comes out, if you can borrow a tampon from any of them. A tampon is 2 ½" long, long enough to reach the torch fluid if the canister is full.

Depending on the size of the Tiki, you might have to trim it with scissors to get it to fit the orifice of the Tiki lid. This is no big deal if it makes your yard look complete for the party.

GARDEN TOOLS - #34

Shovel/Rake/Wheel Barrel Handle Cushion- Mini Pad.

Men, if you live with a female, this application will definitely make you feel better by the end of the day.

All females think they have the right to come up with some hard labor project for us men to do on our days off of work. They think of it as though they're doing us a favor. It always falls on our shoulders to complete this wonderful idea she thought up during the week without asking for your input until she knows exactly what she wants. Then she drops it on you.

Now if you don't go along with this "great" idea of hers, don't plan on getting any action for a while. Know this going into the discussion, ok?

So, once you have agreed with her plans for you for the next couple of days, do what I did, smile and get prepared.

One weekend my girlfriend at the time came up with this great idea to re-landscape the entire backyard before her daughter's graduation party which was to be held in 3 weeks. Ok guys, what do you think I did? You got it. I smiled and asked, "When do <u>we</u> start this great project honey?" She stated, "This week. I'm going to order 18 yards of top soil and 16 yards of mulch."

Now my girlfriend wouldn't be able to help with all this shoveling because she didn't have full use of one of her arms which I pointed out to her. She spun this fact into a positive, by commenting on what great shape I would be in for the party.

When the first 8 yards of top soil hit the drive, I sprung into action with my shovel and wheel barrel. After about an hour, even wearing work gloves, my hands were getting sore. At that moment my sick, warped mind came up with the idea of using her self-adhesive mini pads on the wood handles. I knew by this time into the project where my hands were always positioned on all of the equipment I was using. I went into the house and asked for 6 mini pads. She couldn't argue since I was doing all of heavy labor.

Boy what a difference. I worked until dark that day and my hands did not blister. The next day I added another pad over the old ones and kept on hauling dirt and mulch. This went on for a week with no blisters.

In conclusion, if you have to do hard labor, make it as comfortable as possible.

IV.

Vehicle

Applications

INTERIOR CAR CLEANING - #35

Dash/Instrument Panel Cleaning – Mini Pad.

Adhere a mini pad onto your middle finger (hopefully, you don't have much hair on that finger) then apply glass cleaner to the pad. With your fist clenched, start wiping the panel down. When finished, peel and throw the pad out. If you use a paper towel or rag there is a chance that you will scratch the plastic cover. As males, we wouldn't want our female counterparts to say to us, "you idiot, I can hardly see how much gas is in this thing now that you scratched the "bleep, bleep" out of it".

Guys, mini pads do not have any grit or other abrasive materials in them. They're not called sanitary napkins for nothing! Besides, look how much time you saved by grabbing a mini pad out of the box in the bathroom that we look at every time we're in there. Turn a 10 minute job into a 5 minute one and she'll never miss one mini pad! Oh, and by the way, if you got this far in the manual you should have already gone out and bought her a 6 month supply.

AIR VENT CLEANER - #36

Car/Truck Air Vent Cleaning – Mini Pads.

We've all tried, and most of us have failed, to clean the vents in our vehicle to our satisfaction, right?

I didn't come up with this one, but a female friend of mine did. Take a mini pad and spray whatever you prefer to clean your vents with. You can stick the pad to your hand, or not, but they fit into the slots with ease and they don't leave paper fibers all over as paper towels have a tendency to do. I cleaned my vents by sticking the pad to my index finder and it really works. One mini pad should do the whole vehicle unless you have been off-roading it.

GLOVE BOX PROTECTION - #37

Sunglass Protection While in Glove Box – Mini Pads.

We've all thrown a pair of sunglasses or reading glasses into the glove box just to pull them out to find that they're toast; Scratched to the point they're of no use for reading and, if they're sunglasses, more dangerous to wear than to be blinded by the sun. At this point you think of kicking yourself in the ass. You paid good money for those glasses and didn't have the sense to have your glass case handy before you threw them into the glove box.

Solution: Line the glove box with light day self-adhesive mini pads.

SQUEAKS & RATTLES - #38

Silencing Squeaks & Rattles In Your Vehicle –
Mini Pads Light Days Self-Adhesive.

I don't know how many matchbook covers you've used over the years to stop a squeak or rattle in a vehicle, but I have used my share.

Try this. After locating the contact area of either the squeak or rattle, loosen the piece making contact just enough to be able to slide the mini pad between them. Once you know you have enough clearance remove the pad. Peel the adhesive strip and slide the pad back into place. Tighten the piece back into place and using a razor knife, trim the excess pad flush to the surface. The adhesive will hold the pad in place unlike the matchbook cover that falls out half way through your trip and you're back to square one.

This tip will impress your wife or girlfriend by you being able to fix a concern with a vehicle with something she brought in her purse.

COOKWARE INSULATOR - #39

Cookware/Dinnerware Insulator – Mini Pad.

If you have ever been traveling in a camper or motor home, you probably know of this concern.

A couple years ago my buddies and I rented a motor home to travel to New York State for a national motocross race. It was going to be a 14 to 16 hour drive. We were into the trip for about 45 minutes heading south on I-75 which was very bumpy. It was going on midnight and we were all going nuts due to the rattling coming from the dishes and cookware in the cupboards. We couldn't stand it anymore so we exited in search of a convenience store. We found a gas station and purchased a box of self-adhesive mini pads. We then proceeded to stick one between each plate and pot on board. We had a good laugh at ourselves; 6 male racers sticking mini pads to the plates at 1:00 a.m. on a Friday night.

We headed out again and they were all impressed that I came up with this solution. For this ingenious idea, they let me skip my turn at driving. I was able to watch TV in peace.

It's the little things that can be very irritating on a long trip. This was an emergency fix. The proper fix is to buy the rubber mesh they sell at camper stores but we didn't have that option. By the way, it was a great trip after that concern was eliminated.

FLARE - # 40

Emergency Flare – Tampon.

Tampons can be used for emergency flares as a last resort. Have a box in the trunk of your car along with an extra quart of oil. If stranded and you have no flares, use a tampon by inserting the tampon into the oil while holding onto the string (no oil on hands). Let it soak for 1 minute. The tampon will absorb a lot of fluid. Then using the string, pull the tampon out and light it on fire. Place it in the road as though it was a flare. The oil will burn for approximately 20 minutes. This will give you time to change that flat tire and alert other cars that you are present on the side of the road.

V.

Other

Manly

Applications

FIRE STARTER - #41

Starting a Fire – Tampon.

Guys we've all thrown gas, especially our motorcycle race gas on a fire pit to light the wet wood in the middle of the night. It's midnight and we want to party after the long trip to where we are going to ride for the weekend. Can you relate? If not, you are not a manly man! No, you don't have to race motorcycles to experience this trait. I have a friend that couldn't ride a bicycle let alone a YZ250, but when I came back from a wood run, I realized he was trying to start the fire with my race gas ($4.15 a gallon). I could have killed him because we were miles from any gas station. So, instead of killing my friend, I showed him that if you soak a tampon, preferably a heavy day, in one of the extra quarts of oil, it will burn for 20 minutes. This will allow enough time for the wet twigs to dry and start on fire. Save your race gas for the trails, not the fire pit. By the way, you will still have a quart of oil to change your tranny oil. Tampons absorb a lot of fluid but not so much that you can't use the same quart.

BUCK LURE - #42

Hunting-Buck Lure Instead of Cotton Ball – Tampon.

This past deer season my nephew had buck lure and asked me if I had cotton balls in my cabin. I probably did since females come up once in awhile. We looked in that "magical" top drawer and damn if there weren't a whole bag of them in there.

He used some of my kite string and tied it around the cotton ball which took about 10 minutes. He was going to hang it from the branch where he knew a buck was hanging out. I went with him to put this in the tree and when he went to saturate this cotton ball, he got that crap all over his hands. Believe me he didn't smell like a French whore by any means. Then I thought, "I saw tampons in that drawer". We went back to my cabin and using a piece of string to get enough around a branch, I extended the string and holding the cardboard applicator, pushed it out about a 1/2" and put it on the tampon. This prevents any of that Doe in-heat smell from getting on your hands and making everyone in camp think you need a shower. That stuff doesn't wash off for days, believe me. So I used a tampon and taught a young hunter one lesson that day.

BEER COOLER - #43

Beer Can Wraps – 2 Mini Pads.

Come on guys! What's going to be funnier on a hot summer day than you tossing a cold beer to your buddies with a cool wrap mini pad around it? This should break the tension, if there was any tension between you and your buddies to begin with after the race. Tell him, "At least you didn't double clutch it and tear his arm off in that corner." Have a cold brew with 2 mini pad wraps and tell them to relax, we're only here to have fun and not having to put up with Mr. "P" is why we ran to the woods in the first place, right!"

Don't hit anybody because some manly man will only go home to a female either 2 weeks prior or 2 weeks past of Mr. "P's" visit. We all know us men will feel bad afterward, so strap 2 self-adhesive mini pads around a cold one and have a good laugh.

BOWLING BALL CARE - #44

Bowling Ball Hole Cleaner – Tampon.

Use a tampon to clean the finger holes in your balls. Do not push the tampon fully out of the applicator, just 1" will do. Apply cleaning solution to the end. Work it through the finger holes. When the end is dirty, cut it off and push the remainder of the cleaning swab out.

One tampon can clean 3 balls or 9 finger holes depending on how dirty your balls are.

If you show up at your bowling league with tampons in your bag, this will prove that you are a self-assured manly male. On top of that, give them this tip and see if they too are self-assured manly males. Most males that get caught stealing their wife's or girlfriend's tampons will crumble at that moment, unless they are a self-assured manly male.

DEVIL'S NIGHT PRANK - #45

Teepee a Vehicle/House –
Mini or Maxi Pads/Self-Adhesive.

Do you want to piss a good friend off around Halloween? This is the prank that you should use only on a good friend, if not, you might have a Femi Nazi after your ass.

It's easy to clean up and better than using toilet paper. Buy a box of self-adhesive pads and put them on their vehicle and the windows of their house. You can do this without making noise, except if you're laughing too hard, which my buddy and I did. However, we did not get caught until we confessed 3 years later.

His neighbors thought that he had pissed off a female and she was just retaliating against him. The funniest part of this is he is a self-assured male, races motorcycles and all that stuff. When he opened his bay window and saw mini pads stuck all over it, it was 11:30 in the morning on a Sunday, so 100 plus people had already seen his house like this. That is why it took us 3 years to confess. But get this, when we were on my property riding one weekend, I tossed him a beer with a mini pad wrapped around it and that's when the confession came out.

A THOUGHTFUL GIFT/
TREAT A WOMAN WITH LOVE - #46

Think about it guys, the woman in your life deserves this much from you, don't they? They have to buy them every time Mr. P comes to town.

Save her the trip and buy her at least a 6 month supply of the ones she prefers. Sounds weird, but they will love you more, due to them not having to spend their time and money on them. Be thoughtful you manly men, be self-assured, you have balls, don't you? Prove it, and go buy a supply on your next payday.

Be thankful you don't have to insert a 12 gauge shotgun cleaner up your lower orifice every few weeks. Yes guys, you can buy female hygiene products if you're self-assured.

Guys, take care and love them while you can, because once you've lost them you'll be kicking yourself in the ass. The time you had the opportunity, but thought she was too crabby to give her a hug or to just hold her is the time that she will appreciate you more, knowing that you don't have a motive for your affection.

Don't be selfish, show them your love and affection every day of the year, it will improve your love life by having her know you care and love her no matter if Mr. P is in town or not.

VI.

Health

Applications

BLOODY NOSE - #47

Quick Bloody Nose Fix – Tampon.

I have broken my nose 5 times in my lifetime. Hopefully, I won't break it anymore. When I was snoring, my wife (at that time), requested I see a nose specialist due to me not being able to breathe through my nose anymore. I made the appointment and when we were waiting to see the doctor, to my dismay, my nose was bleeding profusely. In came the prettiest, little Polish doctor and she proceeded to shove, what looked like a tampon, up my right nostril. I haven't been that abused by a female since a female doctor gave me a vasectomy. Hey guys, a vasectomy isn't too bad. The girls you date put it in the "asset" column of things they like about you. Remember our goal is to want women to like or love us for who we are. Go figure.

So anyways, a light day tampon will stop the bleeding but, I wouldn't go out in public with a string hanging out of my nose. An extra tip with this one: Put a little Vaseline on it before insertion. This also helps when pulling it out.

Guys, you won't believe this, I broke my nose again before I finished the final version of this book. I left the big city life of Detroit and came to Pinedale, Wyoming to become a wrangler in the Rocky mountains. On my 7th day in the Rocky mountains, we were going to go to a base camp by horse back. The six of us got to the trail head and Dustin, (our guide), tells me to ride this new horse that nobody has ridden before in our camp. Needless to say, it was fine until I mounted it, then all hell broke loose and it began to buck, at which time, 3 or 4 bucks later, my face met his head and I found myself on the ground. Bleeding bad I asked the girl in our group for a tampon and to take a picture. She took the picture, but had no tampons. I used toilet paper to keep the blood under control while being driven to Pinedale Medical. This goes to show, you should keep some tampons in your saddle bags.

The personnel at the Pinedale clinic treated me better than I've ever been treated before by a medical facility. Here's the kicker, they were out of nose tampons! They knew exactly what I was talking about and then proceeded to shove rolled up gauze up my nose. I mentioned this book to them and told them I would give them a shout out in it. I shouldn't have, since they sent me a $600.00 bill for their services, but what the hell.

I was back on a horse in a day and continued my adventures in the Rockies with feminine products in my saddle bags. Oh, by the way, they keep maxi pads in the horses' first aid kit to use as gauze in case a horse gets cut. Even these wranglers in the mountains keep these products on hand, go figure!

EYE PROTECTION - #48

Eye Protection From The Sun – Mini Pad.

This one can be used by males or females, and may seem a bit weird but it does keep your eye lids from being burnt. It can also be comical at the same time. If you don't have those plastic, strap on eye protectors handy and you don't want to spend the $5/$10 they're asking for at the front desk (that's the cost of a beer), do this. If you have a female companion with you, ask her for a mini pad. Cut it into the shape of your eyes. Now here's the comical part; before you peel off the adhesive strip, write something on the front of it. If you're at the beach, who cares what statement you put on it. Have fun!

A girl I came across on an island had burnt her eye lids bad, but didn't want to put a towel across her entire face. I told her this would work. This isn't one of my original ideas. I saw it at a motorcycle race where a group of guys had them on with statements I can't write in this book. Thanks Hill People.

ANKLE/KNEE BRACE PAD - #49

Brace Pad Ankle/Knee – Mini Pad.

I am one of the millions that wear a knee brace on occasion. When I rode, my knee brace padding was pretty worn out on the inside and rubbing against the gas tank didn't help either. I took a mini pad out of my motocross gear bag and stuck it to the area of irritation. It worked. That is why I keep a supply handy. You're not going to get your brace fixed on a weekend in the middle of no where, so this will keep the skin on your knee for the weekend.

One of my past girlfriends wore an ankle brace everyday. One day her brace was rubbing to the point that it rubbed a patch of skin off the back of her ankle. I thought about the mini pad fix and proceeded to adhere 2 mini pads onto her brace. This was something that impressed her and she was in a much better mood the rest of that day.

GAUZE - #50

Emergency Gauze – Mini or Maxi Pad.

A lot of people freak at the sight of someone bleeding bad especially out in the middle of nowhere, but not me. I used this one on my cousin, Paul Hayes, who split his side open riding one weekend on a washout downhill trail. The good thing was that I got to see the whole thing and laughed like hell after I knew he wasn't seriously hurt.

So we're 20 miles from the Cadillac General Hospital and 3 miles from my cabin. We went back to the cabin and I went into the famous "drawer". There I retrieved a maxi pad and a roll of duct tape. We placed the maxi pad on the wound and duct taped it in place until we could get him to the hospital for stitches.

The nurse had never seen a person come into emergency with a maxi pad taped on their body, but she stated it was a smart thing to do. He was fine, but was unable to ride for the rest of that weekend.

VII.

The

Tampon

Bouquet

ATTRACTIVE STORAGE OF FEMALE HYGIENE PRODUCTS.

BONUS: ALL PRODUCTS APPLY

This is one I've used for 20 or more years. I got tired of looking at that tampon or mini pad box on the bathroom shelf or floor, so I came up with a solution. I took a silver (cheap) vase and put all the hygiene products in it. I named it the "Tampon Bouquet". I placed all the panty shields, tampons, and assorted pads all in one nice vase. It is shaped more like a bowl. A little advice, don't put them in a tall vase because you'll look like an idiot. Place it on the top shelf if you have one, and any female that is over your place will either think you're a self-assured male or a guy that really gets around. Hopefully, the first will come to the mind.

I don't care how manly you are; just seeing those boxes are a turn off even if Mr. P. is four weeks away.

Women show appreciation with these little things even if they don't comment on them. Every guy hates to see a tampon box looking him in the face every time he relieves himself, right? Make one in the next 15 minutes and throw that box out of the bathroom and the next trip to lift the lid, you'll laugh. Laugh, life is short.

VIII.

Closing

IN CLOSING

While writing this manual and sharing my warped ideas on the uses of these sometimes uncomfortable objects laying around our homes, it occurred to me that I have opened the eyes of men in a totally different way on how we can use something we have always shied away from.

I've laughed out loud on numerous occasions while writing down these weird applications for these products. I also realize that a hell of a lot of you are thinking I'm a very strange and sick individual. Well in some aspects of my mind you are probably right. You have to admit though there are ones you will be using. So who is the sick individual now?

I have always loved to make people laugh and I've been told I can remember and tell a hell of a lot of dirty, as well as clean, jokes. More people have to stop taking this time on planet Earth so seriously and have more laughter in their lives.

This manual was written with this philosophy in mind. I hope it made you laugh or at least brought a smile to your face. One of my main goals with my time here is to make as many people have some laughter in their souls.

Thank you for the precious time it took you to read this manual and keep your eyes open for Volume II – Another 50 Ways to Use Feminine Hygiene Products For the Self-Assured Male.

Just B. Koz

Lightning Source UK Ltd.
Milton Keynes UK
08 December 2010
164115UK00001B/35/P